Animals Working Together

Clown Fish and Sea Anemones Work Together

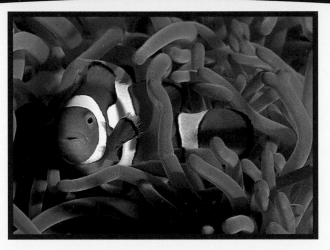

by Martha E. H. Rustad

Consulting Editor: Gail Saunders-Smith, PhD

Consultant: Jackie Gai, DVM
Zoo and Exotic Animal Consultation

CAPSTONE PRESS
a capstone imprint

Pebble Plus is published by Capstone Press,
1710 Roe Crest Drive, North Mankato, Minnesota 56003.
www.capstonepub.com

Library of Congress Cataloging-in-Publication Data
Rustad, Martha E. H. (Martha Elizabeth Hillman), 1975–
  Clown fish and sea anemones work together / by Martha E. H. Rustad.
    p. cm.—(Pebble plus. Animals working together)
  Includes bibliographical references and index.
  Summary: "Simple text and full-color photographs introduces the symbiotic relationship of clown fish and sea anemones"—Provided by publisher.
  ISBN 978-1-4296-5297-1 (library binding)
  ISBN 978-1-4296-6198-0 (paperback)
  1. Anemonefishes—Ecology—Juvenile literature. 2. Sea anemones—Ecology—Juvenile literature. 3. Symbiosis—Juvenile literature. I. Title. II. Series.
  QL638.P77R867 2011
  597'.7—dc22
                                                                    2010025462

Editorial Credits
Erika L. Shores, editor; Bobbie Nuytten, designer; Svetlana Zhurkin, media researcher;
    Laura Manthe, production specialist

Photo Credits
Alamy/Stephen Frink Collection, 18–19
Brand X Pictures, 1
Digital Vision, 11
Dreamstime/Exploretimor, cover, 20–21; Jose Manuel Gelpi Diaz, 4–5; Olga Khoroshunova, 12–13
Photodisc, 6–7
Shutterstock/Rich Carey, 15; Tatiana Belova, 9; Tyler Fox, 16–17

Note to Parents and Teachers

The Animals Working Together series supports national science standards related to biology. This book describes and illustrates the relationship between clown fish and sea anemones. The images support early readers in understanding the text. The repetition of words and phrases helps early readers learn new words. This book also introduces early readers to subject-specific vocabulary words, which are defined in the Glossary section. Early readers may need assistance to read some words and to use the Table of Contents, Glossary, Read More, Internet Sites, and Index sections of the book.

Table of Contents

Symbiosis

A clown fish swims near
a coral reef. Sea anemone
tentacles wiggle nearby. The fish
darts into the stinging tentacles.
Is the fish in danger?

The clown fish is safe.

Stings from sea anemones

do not hurt clown fish.

Slimy mucus covers clown fish

scales and protects it from stings.

Sea anemones and clown fish are animal partners. Each helps the other find food, shelter, and safety. This relationship is called symbiosis.

Sea Anemones Help Clown Fish

Clown fish stay safe

in sea anemones.

Clown fish hide from predators

in anemone tentacles.

Clown Fish Help Sea Anemones

Sea anemones attach to reefs.

Their stinging tentacles wait

for fish, shrimp, and other prey.

Clown fish lure prey to sea anemones. Clown fish swim through the tentacles. Other fish think the sea anemone is safe and get stung.

Clown fish eat parasites and leftover food scraps on anemones. Clown fish get food, and the anemones stay clean and healthy.

Predators such as butterfly fish try to eat anemones. Clown fish click their teeth to scare away predators.

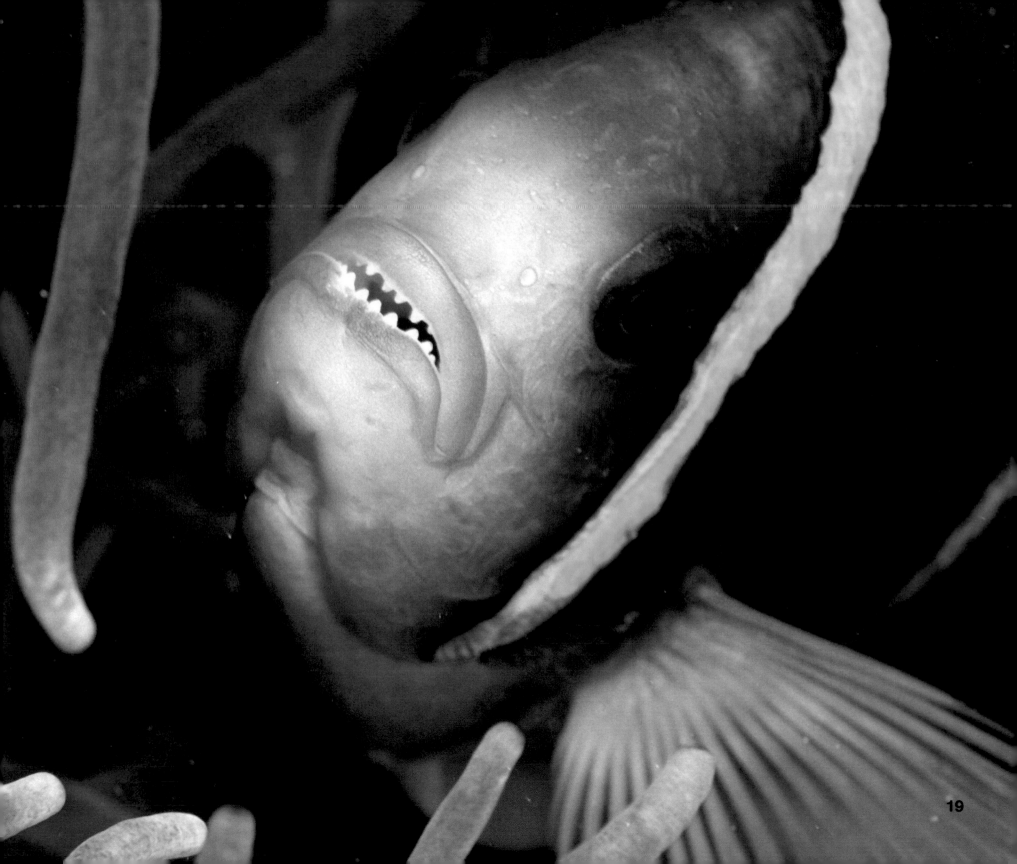

Teamwork

On a busy coral reef,

clown fish and sea anemones

are a team. Symbiosis keeps

both animals healthy and safe.

Glossary

coral reef—an area of coral skeletons and rocks in shallow ocean water

lure—to try to get something to come closer

mucus—a slimy, thick liquid

parasite—a small organism that lives on or inside an animal or person; parasites sometimes hurt the animal it lives on or inside

scale—one of the small, thin plates that covers the bodies of fish

sting—to hurt with a poisoned tip; sea anemones sting prey with their tentacles

symbiosis—a relationship between two different kinds of animals; the animals live together to help each other find food, shelter, or safety

tentacle—a long, flexible arm of an animal; sea anemones sting prey with their tentacles

Read More

Levy, Janey. *Discovering Coral Reefs.* World Habitats. New York : Rosen Pub. Group's PowerKids Press, 2008.

Rake, Jody Sullivan. *Sea Anemones.* Under the Sea. Mankato, Minn.: Capstone Press, 2006.

Silverman, Buffy. *You Scratch My Back.* Raintree Fusion. Chicago: Raintree, 2008.

Internet Sites

FactHound offers a safe, fun way to find Internet sites related to this book. All of the sites on FactHound have been researched by our staff.

Here's all you do:

Visit *www.facthound.com*

Type in this code: 9781429652971

 Check out projects, games and lots more at **www.capstonekids.com**

Index

Word Count: 185
Grade: 1
Early-Intervention Level: 17